A Content Analysis of the Cable News Network and the Three Broadcast Networks

CNN vs THE NETWORKS: Is More News Better News?

With a Foreword by Patrick D. Maines

Media Research Series

the media institute

Washington, D.C.

CNN vs. the Networks:
Is More News Better News?

Copyright © 1983 The Media Institute

All rights reserved. No part of this publication may be reproduced or transmitted in any form without permission in writing from the publisher.

First printing December 1983.
Second printing December 1983.

Published by The Media Institute, Washington, D.C.

Printed in the United States of America.

ISBN: 0-937790-23-0

Library of Congress Catalog Card Number: 83-63260

Table of Contents

		Page
	Foreword	v
	Executive Summary and Conclusions	ix
I.	Introduction	1
II.	Findings	7
III.	Comparison of the Broadcast Networks	23
IV.	Background and Attitudes Survey of CNN Personnel	31
V.	Appendix	39

Foreword

The advent of the Cable News Network, the country's first all-news cable television system, offered up from the beginning the prospect of dramatic improvement in both the quantity and quality of televised news to the nation.

Whereas the broadcast networks are limited, in all but the most compelling circumstances, to program formats which present hard news only at the news hour, CNN has the capability of going "live" at any time of the day or night with breaking stories, be they modest or momentous. Much more importantly, by being an all-news network, CNN has the capability of transmitting vastly more news than its broadcast competition, thus greatly freeing it from the time constraints that broadcasters have referred to as the "tyranny of the clock."

Finally, by operating within one of the new technologies--cable TV--CNN brings with it the promise of a dramatic new means of telecommunication; one that might provide extraordinary diversity, and by doing so entice millions of new viewers to the televideo revolution.

For us at The Media Institute, possibilities such as these are of more than a passing interest. Since its founding in 1979, the Institute has closely monitored and analyzed television news coverage, specifically that focusing on business and economic issues, and has too often found such coverage to be greatly deficient. Thus it was that in early 1982 we decided to conduct a comparative study of the business and economic coverage of CNN and the broadcast networks.

From the beginning we determined that our methodological approach would be a "content analysis," a research technique we had used many times in the past in other studies. We were drawn to this technique for the reason that it can provide unique and replicable insights, and because we were unaware of the existence of any other methodologically rigorous studies of CNN, or indeed of any of the programming offered by the new technologies, other than anecdotal studies of dubious validity.

While a fuller statement of the methodology is given later in this report, a few comments might be in order. First, we were determined that the study be a <u>comparative</u> study of CNN and its broadcast competition, and this determination brought us immediately to our first problem: what to compare and how to compare it? Here we had CNN, which broadcasts news 24 hours a day, and the three broadcast networks which, even including such "soft news" programs as <u>60 Minutes</u>, give over only a fraction of that amount of time to their news departments. Our approach to the resolution of this problem was two-fold: First, we decided to analyze just the "flagship" hard-news programs offered by CNN and the networks (the nightly news programs of ABC, CBS, and NBC, and <u>Primenews</u>, a two-hour nightly program on CNN); and second, and precisely because <u>Primenews</u> was a two-hour program while the network offerings were only half-hour programs, we decided to analyze all data in terms <u>relative</u> to the time available on each program.

Our second major concern was that the standards of performance measured not be divisible by political or ideological considerations. We did not want to determine whether CNN or the networks were pro- or anti-Reagan, nor did we want to determine whether they were pro- or anti-Big Business, conservative or liberal. Rather, we wanted to create measurements of standards of performance that people of differing political and ideological viewpoints would recognize as objective and satisfactory. In meeting this concern, we carefully reviewed the literature of media criticism issuing from all quarters, and selected four tests of performance: balance, depth, sensationalism, and news priority.

Of course, it should be acknowledged here that none of the disciplines of the social sciences (much less the techniques used within those disciplines) can ever fully apprehend the whole picture, or the whole "truth," of any given entity or circumstance. On the other hand, and as someone once said, there is a difference between a lack of complete knowledge and a complete lack of knowledge. We believe that both our approach and our findings--while certainly not the last word on this subject--represent a significant and valid set of insights into the questions we investigated.

More than this, we are especially pleased to be the first organization to raise up for public scrutiny the performance of one of the first and most successful of the program services operating within a new communications technology. For us this will be just the first of numerous activities, including other studies, seminars, and workshops, focusing on the new and the old technologies, and on the regulatory and legal deliberations that will have such a major impact on their future.

That on balance CNN does indeed outperform its broadcast competition--which is one of the two major conclusions of this study--is a thing in which people inside CNN and the whole of the cable industry might take pride. That there is no absolute correlation between broadcast time and program quality--which is the second major conclusion, based in important measure on the extraordinary performance of ABC vis-a-vis its broadcast competition--might be a thing of some pride to ABC, and an example to the whole of the broadcast industry that the future need not belong solely to the new technologies.

Patrick D. Maines
President
The Media Institute
November 1983

Executive Summary and Conclusions

The advent of the Cable News Network (CNN) prompted many observers to wonder if more news would also mean better news, i.e. would CNN's freedom from the 22-minute news format allow it to produce news programming that was qualitatively better than that of the three major networks. To help answer this question, The Media Institute undertook a comparative study of the networks' nightly evening newscasts and CNN's equivalent of these, a two-hour evening program called Primenews.
 In particular, the study examined the domestic business and economic news stories that appeared in over 37 hours of news time on CNN, ABC, CBS, and NBC during the summer and fall of 1982. (It should be noted that the study looked only at nightly evening newscasts, and not at other general or business-oriented news programs on CNN or the networks.) Using a research technique known as content analysis, the study employed multiple measures to discover if there were significant differences between the business and economic coverage of CNN and the networks, according to four criteria: (1) balance; (2) sensationalism; (3) depth; and (4) priority. The viewing periods happened to coincide with two major economic events: the stock-market rally in August 1982,

and passage of a major tax-increase bill, also in August.

FINDINGS

Overall, the study finds that CNN's business and economic reporting was more balanced and less sensational than that of the networks (i.e. the average of ABC, CBS, and NBC). However, CNN's coverage was of less depth than network coverage (relative to the time available), despite the two-hour format of Primenews. The news priorities of CNN and the networks did not differ significantly. Of specific interest are the following differences:

Balance
CNN was more balanced than the networks in its business and economic coverage, relying on a wider variety of sources and presenting a more balanced mix of viewpoints on a controversial economic issue.*
* As a percentage of the total time devoted to sources, CNN relied markedly less on government sources than did the networks (CNN 38%, networks 47%).
* CNN relied less than half as much as the networks on "men-in-the-street" as sources of information (CNN 8%, networks 17%).
* CNN relied on economists as sources four times

---

* Researchers assumed that coverage relying on a mix of sources (e.g. government, industry and labor spokesmen, economists, etc.) was more balanced than coverage relying too heavily on one source (which in practice is usually the government). Similarly, researchers felt that the use of men-in-the-street as sources diminished balance insofar as it reduced the time available for a mix of informed sources.

more than did the networks, as a percentage of the total time devoted to sources (CNN 12%, networks 3%).
* In covering a major tax-increase bill, CNN presented a more balanced mix of pro- and anti-tax bill viewpoints than did the networks (CNN 58% pro, 26% anti, 16% neutral; networks 72% pro, 16% anti, 12% neutral).

Sensationalism
CNN's business and economic coverage was less sensational than that of the networks, according to two measures.
* The first sentences of CNN's lead stories were judged less sensational than the networks' by independent research subjects, using a social-science research technique known as a Q-Sort.
* The networks used "case studies," i.e. told a story in terms of how a development affected one individual or group**, twice as often as did CNN, relative to their total business and economic news time (CNN 5%, networks 10%).

Depth
CNN's coverage was generally of less depth than the networks', according to three measures.
* A greater percentage of economic terms with complex or unclear meanings were defined in network stories than in CNN stories (CNN 7%, networks 17%).
* CNN discussed the causes and implications of the stock-market rally less than did the networks, as a percentage of business and economic news time (CNN 31%, networks 39%).

** Case studies were seen to contribute to sensationalism insofar as they were generally emotional in nature, and reduced the time available for objective, disinterested reporting of the actual event.

* CNN spent a slightly higher percentage of the time it devoted to the tax bill in discussing the bill's provisions (CNN 2%, networks 1%). But most of its coverage, like the networks, dealt with political alliances, ideological controversies and vote counts.

News Priority

No significant differences were found between CNN and the networks regarding the priority placed on business and economic news.
* CNN devoted slightly less of its total news time to business and economic issues than did the networks (CNN 20%, networks 23%).
* CNN ranked a domestic business or economic news story first, second, or third slightly more often than did the networks, but not often enough to be significant (CNN 17 times, network average 13 times).

Comparison Among the Three Broadcast Networks

Although the primary purpose of the study was to compare CNN's coverage with network averages of coverage, researchers discovered several very important differences among the three network newscasts. In general, ABC substantially outperformed CBS and NBC as measured by the study's four criteria; in fact, had the study compared only ABC and CNN, the outcome might have been much closer.
* ABC devoted 48% more time to domestic business and economic issues than did NBC, and 18% more time than CBS.
* ABC devoted twice the amount of time to economists as sources than CBS, and slightly more than NBC.
* ABC used business/industry representatives twice the amount of time that either CBS or NBC did.
* ABC spent over twice the amount of time discussing the causes and implications of the stock-market rally than either CBS or NBC did.

Survey of CNN Personnel

This report also contains the results of a survey of CNN news personnel, which the Institute conducted to determine whether cable journalists differ from their broadcast counterparts in their backgrounds and attitudes toward business and economics. The Institute was unable to include personnel from the three networks in the survey, because the networks refused to furnish the names of appropriate staff. Instead, researchers used data from an earlier survey, "Media and Business Elites," by S. Robert Lichter and Stanley Rothman.

In their study of 240 print and broadcast journalists at the most influential media outlets, Lichter and Rothman ascertained the attitudes of these so-called "media elite" on a variety of social and political issues. The Institute's survey replicated their questions on economic attitudes and social goals, and included additional questions related to economic attitudes.

* Like the media elite, the CNN respondents were well educated; the average CNN respondent had over 10 years of experience in the news media.

* CNN personnel more strongly agreed with free-market attitudes and more strongly disagreed with attitudes that favored government intervention, than did the journalists surveyed by Lichter and Rothman.

* CNN personnel more strongly favored goals such as a stable economy, economic growth, and the fight against crime; the media elite more strongly favored goals such as a more humane society, placing ideas ahead of money, and beautifying cities and countryside.

* CNN journalists generally displayed social values that were markedly more conservative than their media-elite counterparts--values that were, in fact, very much in tune with those of corporate executives surveyed by Lichter and Rothman.

CONCLUSIONS

(1) It appears that the business and economic news coverage of CNN's nightly news program is generally superior to the average of comparable network coverage. According to the criteria used in this study, CNN coverage was found to be more balanced and less sensational, and roughly comparable to the networks in terms of depth and news priority. Because CNN surpassed network averages in the important categories of balance and sensationalism, and performed similarly in the other categories, The Media Institute assesses that CNN's coverage was superior overall.

Among the three broadcast networks, ABC was clearly superior in its business and economic news coverage, as measured by the total amount of time devoted to these issues, balance and diversity of news sources, and depth of coverage. Anecdotal evidence suggests that ABC and CNN might, in fact, be close rivals, but more study is needed on this topic.

As it turns out, there is no simple answer to our original research question, "Is more news better news?" It is possible to say, "Yes, CNN business and economic news is better, but not necessarily because there is more of it." CNN news coverage was more balanced, and indeed CNN took advantage of its additional time to present a better-balanced mix of news sources and opinions. However, balance correlates only moderately with time available; editorial judgments play a large role as well.

CNN also surpassed the networks by being less sensational, and sensationalism is not a function of time available. Thus, we must look again to other factors, such as the judgments of editors, the skills of writers, and the structures of news organizations, to explain this difference; however, such an analysis is not within the scope of this study. Likewise, news priority is not a function of time available, and it is not surprising that CNN and the networks exhibit roughly the same priorities.

What _is_ surprising, however, is that CNN displayed less depth of coverage. This is the one area where we would have expected CNN to take advantage of additional time to discuss complex business and economic issues in significantly greater detail. But in some ways the networks--long accused of superficiality--covered these issues in more depth.

Thus, CNN excelled in balance but lagged in depth, even though CNN's additional time could have been expected to yield at least some qualitative improvement in _both_ of these time-sensitive areas. Meanwhile, CNN outperformed the networks by being less sensational, and demonstrated about the same news priorities as the networks. But neither sensationalism nor news priority is related to time available; therefore, CNN's superior performance in sensationalism must be the result of factors not related to time.

This suggests the broader conclusion: <u>(2) The quality of television business and economic news depends only in part on the amount of time available.</u> CNN has shown clearly, for example, that news can be conveyed without the degree of sensationalism commonly found on the networks; yet at the same time, CNN has not seemed to meet its potential for in-depth coverage. Or viewed another way, the networks are offering depth of coverage that is comparable to CNN, relatively speaking, despite their abbreviated formats. That time is only one factor affecting quality is confirmed by the comparison among the broadcast networks, which finds the quality of ABC's coverage far exceeds that of the other two networks--even though all three have 22-minute formats.

What, then, accounts for the difference? At bottom it is probably editorial policies, day-to-day news judgments and other factors that determine content, and therefore quality. CNN demonstrates that time _can_ be an advantage, especially in establishing balance; it can also be an advantage missed, as in the case of depth.

<u>Paradoxically, CNN succeeds best in the areas that have little or no relation to newscast length</u>. And herein lies an important lesson for the networks: "not enough time" is no longer an excuse for unbalanced and sensational coverage; nor will more time automatically improve the quality of coverage. For as the Cable News Network has shown, quality is a factor of more than mere program length.

I. Introduction

The nightly news programs of the three television networks have been targets of criticism from many quarters, and for many reasons. But perhaps one description comes closest to capturing the character of TV news as we have known it: "a struggle against superficiality."1

Critics have been especially vocal in citing the shortcomings of the networks in their coverage of business topics, and of economic issues. However, complaints of imbalanced, shallow, and sensationalized coverage have been dismissed with the response that the 22-minute newscast is, by its very nature, little more than a headline service; thus, the argument goes, network news should not be expected to do justice to business and economic issues that are complex, and (at least until the advent of computer graphics) not well suited for visual depiction.

"A half-hour news show, reduced to type, fills only half the front page of a standard-sized daily newspaper, necessitating the omission of many important stories and the compression of those

---

1 A. Kent MacDougall, "TV Coverage is Struggle Against Superficiality," Los Angeles Times, February 5, 1980.

that make the air to the point where comprehension is often sacrificed."2

Because this shortage of time is generally regarded as a major cause of the networks' inadequate business and economic reporting, we asked this logical question: Would more time ensure better reporting of domestic business and economic issues?

In seeking the answer to this question, we turned to a communications medium that is currently providing the viewing public with more news: cable television. Over 30 million homes (or about one out of three homes with TV sets) currently subscribe to cable TV, making it the most widely available of the new communications technologies. Of these, almost 22 million homes receive the one cable channel airing extended-length news programs 24 hours per day: Cable News Network (CNN). CNN airs 19 different news programs each weekday, 35 on Saturday and 36 on Sunday.

Headquartered in Atlanta, CNN had, at the time of this study, approximately 450 staff members operating out of 13 domestic and seven foreign bureaus. From the beginning of its news day at 6 a.m., CNN airs a variety of programming, including shows oriented toward sports, business, and medical news. While "hard news" shows and spots recur throughout the day, the bulk of CNN's hard-news programming runs from 8-10 p.m. EST.

SCOPE OF THE STUDY

For a number of reasons, this study is limited to an analysis of the domestic business and economic news stories appearing on the nightly newscasts of CNN and the three broadcast networks. In the case of ABC, CBS, and NBC, these are the 30-minute early-evening newscasts, while for CNN the equivalent of these is a two-hour news program

---

[2] Ibid.

called <u>Primenews</u>, shown between 8-10 p.m. EST. It should be noted that this study looks <u>only</u> at nightly evening newscasts, and not at other general or business-oriented news programs on these networks. CNN, for example, has a regular 30-minute weeknight program devoted to business and economic news, <u>Moneyline</u>. Obviously, for those viewers with a particular interest in business and economic news, <u>Moneyline</u> could fulfill their needs far better than any general news program, broadcast or cable. The same could also be said of <u>Money Week</u>, CNN's twice-weekly, 30-minute review of business, economic, and financial developments, and <u>Inside Business</u>, a weekly hour-long interview program with corporate leaders.

However, our goal was to conduct a comparative study, and we were therefore limited to that which could be compared. The other programs on CNN, such as <u>Moneyline</u>, could not be included in the study because they lacked broadcast counterparts. Likewise, we did not attempt to include the networks' newly added late-night and early-morning news shows, Sunday morning interview shows or magazine-style shows like <u>60 Minutes</u>. The study compares only the "flagship" general news programs of CNN and the networks, focusing specifically on the business and economic news coverage in these programs. And indeed, it is from these general news shows that the largest audiences receive the majority of televised information about business and economic issues. Thus, these newscasts merit study in their own right. As a result, this analysis does not attempt to draw conclusions about <u>all</u> business and economic news available on CNN and the networks throughout the day, or to generalize about the merits of CNN vs. network performance based on more than their nightly evening newscasts.

Three weeks of newscasts in 1982 were selected for analysis: August 16-20, October 4-8, and November 8-12. However, August 16 was dropped from the analysis because almost the entire <u>Prime-</u>

news program that day was devoted to a presidential address. It was felt that inclusion of this program might distort the findings.

Researchers identified a total of 145 business and economic stories on CNN and 167 stories on the networks. Some of these "stories," however, were merely statistics (e.g. the Dow Jones Industrial Average) shown briefly on the screen. These were included in total time tallies but excluded from the content analysis. As a result, 143 CNN stories and 122 network stories were used for the content analysis.

Business and economic news stories totalled 4 hours, 32 minutes and 10 seconds for CNN, and 3 hours, 37 minutes and 2 seconds for the three broadcast networks.

Four topics accounted for over half of the business and economic news on CNN and the networks: unemployment, the tax-increase bill, the stock-market rally, and social security. (See Table 1.)

SUMMARY OF METHODOLOGY

This study employed an objective and reliable media research technique known as content analy-

Table 1.

Business/Economic News Time Devoted to Major Topics (%)

	ABC	CBS	NBC	CNN
Unemployment	22%	22%	28%	16%
Tax-Increase Bill	17%	17%	22%	9%
Stock-Market Rally	21%	16%	12%	14%
Social Security	8%	8%	6%	12%
	68%	63%	68%	51%

sis. Briefly stated, content analysis is a systematic technique for organizing communication content into various categories.

Story Selection

Researchers arrived at a preliminary list of 140 business and economic news topics, relying on abstracts and indexes published by the Vanderbilt Television News Archive, and the viewing, abstracting, and indexing of <u>Primenews</u> videotapes. The Vanderbilt Television News Archive compiled videotapes of selected network stories, while CNN provided videotapes of <u>Primenews</u> programs. Forty-seven business and economic news categories were actually represented in these tapes. (For a list of the 47 categories see Appendix.) Specially trained "coders" viewed the videotapes three separate times and recorded data on prepared code sheets.

Criteria

The study set out to assess network performance based on four major research criteria: balance, sensationalism, depth, and news priority. Each major criterion was measured using at least two key tests.

<u>Balance</u> was determined by analyzing the types of sources used in stories and their diversity; and by studying the balance of opposing viewpoints presented on one major economic topic, the tax-increase bill.

<u>Sensationalism</u> was determined by using a Q-Sort test, in which individuals were asked to rank the first sentences of lead stories according to their perceived sensationalism. Sensationalism was also measured by studying the number and type (positive, negative, or neutral) of "case studies," <u>i.e.</u> stories that told how a policy or development affected one individual.

Depth was measured by studying how frequently economic terms with complex or unclear meanings were defined in business and economic news stories. Depth was also determined by evaluating the amount of time spent discussing the causes and implications of the stock-market rally, and specific provisions of the tax-increase bill.

Priority was determined by comparing the percentage of newscast time devoted to business and economic issues, and the rank or position of such stories in the newscast.

*   *   *

Any comparative study of two different media is, from the beginning, plagued by seeming limitations. One such question facing this study at its outset was, "How can more be compared with less?," especially because the most objective and quantifiable tool available to the television researcher is the measurement of time. It was assumed that CNN would devote more absolute time to business and economic issues because it had more time available. However, the objective of the study was not to determine, tautologically speaking, if more news was more news. Rather, its goal was to assess whether more news is better news: more balanced, less sensational, of greater depth, and with a greater priority on business and economic stories.

Therefore, to overcome the problem of comparing more with less (two hours versus 30 minutes), researchers analyzed study data consistently in percentage terms. Data was analyzed as a percentage of general evening news time available on CNN compared to time available on the networks, as a percentage of time CNN and the networks devoted to a particular variable, etc. While the study measured each variable in absolute time, the data presented in the following chapters represent relative time, or time as a percentage of a given total.

II. Findings

The findings of this study may surprise some observers, for they suggest that CNN does, in fact, surpass the networks[3] in reporting business and economic news according to two important criteria: balance and sensationalism. Perhaps equally surprising, however, is the finding that CNN's coverage does not offer significantly greater depth than do the networks, when measured as a percentage of available time. Likewise, the news priorities of CNN and the networks do not differ significantly. Below are the findings for each of the four major research criteria.

BALANCE

The most dramatic difference between CNN and the networks was found in the area of balance, and

---

[3] Unless otherwise noted, all references to the "networks" refer to the <u>averages</u> of data for ABC, CBS, and NBC. Data were collected for each network (and are summarized in the following chapter), but were averaged to meet the objective of the study: a comparison between the business and economic coverage of CNN and that of the networks in general.

specifically in CNN's use of sources. Not only did CNN give more time, relatively speaking, to a wider variety of sources, but it also presented a more balanced mix of opposing viewpoints on a particularly divisive economic issue: the tax-increase bill.

Diversity of Sources

Of fundamental importance is the finding that CNN relied less on government sources of information than did the broadcast networks--in fact, the networks relied on government sources 24% more. An overreliance on government sources, to the exclusion of other types of sources, has been an all-too-frequent characteristic of broadcast coverage.[4] In this study, researchers assumed that coverage relying on a mix of sources, e.g. government, industry and labor spokesmen, economists, etc., is more balanced than coverage relying too heavily on one source--which in practice is usually the government. Thus, the fact that CNN relies markedly less on government sources distinguishes it from the networks.

Of no less importance is that CNN relied substantially less on an average citizen or "man-in-the-street" as a source of information. The broadcast networks relied on a man-in-the-street as a source 17% of the total time devoted to sources, while CNN relied on this type of source 8%--less than half as much. While some may argue that an average citizen's reaction to an event is itself newsworthy, in reality more time devoted to "men-in-the-street" means less time devoted to informed sources of information. The use of men-in-the-street does not, prima facie, denote imbalance. But it can diminish balance insofar as

---

[4] Leonard J. Theberge, ed., TV Coverage of the Oil Crises: How Well Was the Public Served? (Washington, D.C.: The Media Institute, 1982).

it reduces the time available for a mix of informed sources.

CNN relied more heavily than did the networks on two other types of informed sources: economists and business/industry representatives. CNN called on economists 12% of the total time devoted to sources--four times more than the networks, which used economists 3% of the time. CNN called on business and industry representatives 12% of the time, compared to the networks' 8%. No differences were observed between CNN and the networks in the percentage of time devoted to labor leaders and experts (a category that included academics and financial analysts, but excluded economists and business/industry representatives)--4% and 19%, respectively. (See Chart 1.)

One startling finding is that almost two-thirds more of the business and economic news on CNN could be attributed to outside, identifiable sources. On CNN, 41% of business and economic news time could be attributed to a source, com-

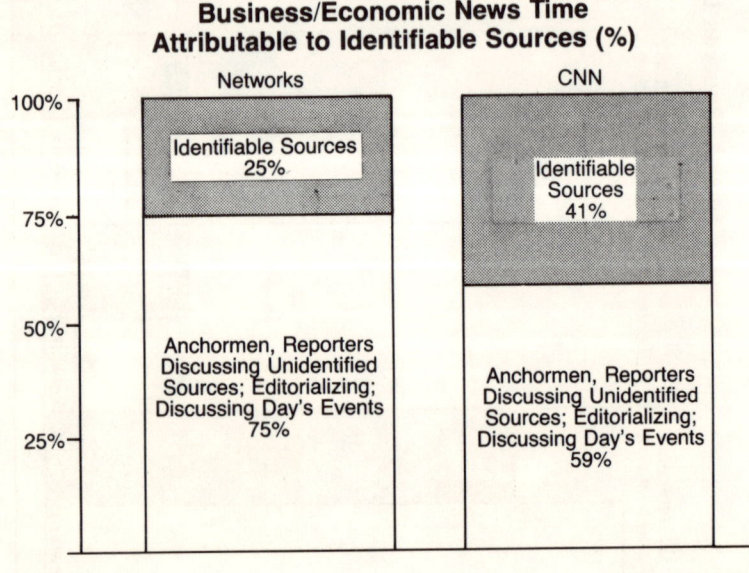

Chart 2.
Business/Economic News Time
Attributable to Identifiable Sources (%)

pared to 25% of that time on the networks. (See Chart 2.) In practice, this meant that CNN devoted less time to an anchor or reporter discussing the statements of unidentified sources, or editorializing, or simply describing the day's events.

Tax-Increase Bill

As a second and different measure of "balance," the study focused on one issue that received substantial coverage on CNN and the networks during the viewing period: President Reagan's $96-billion tax-increase bill. (This tax-<u>increase</u> proposal followed the President's earlier tax cut.) This bill proved to be a useful measure of balance, because opinion on it cut sharply across party lines in a way that defied typical pro- and anti-administration sentiment--and hence coverage. Researchers measured the amount of time given to sources who supported and opposed passage of the

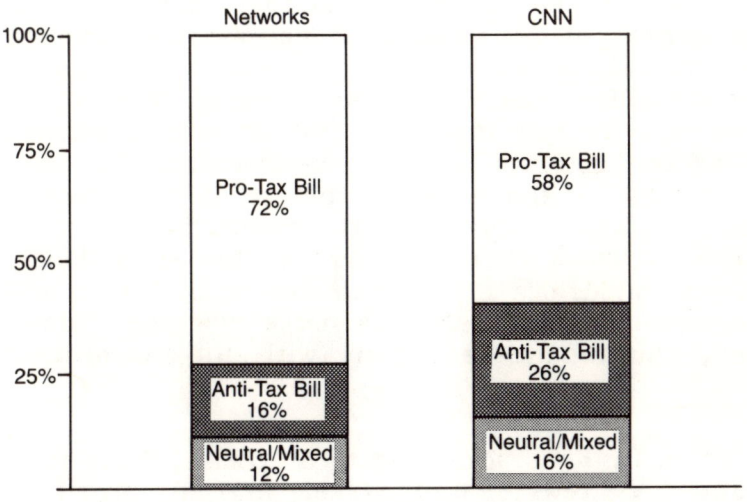

**Chart 3.
Viewpoints of Sources Used in Tax-Bill Stories (%)**

bill, as well as those who had no identifiable position.

Sources on both CNN and the networks favored passage of the tax bill a majority of the time, but significantly less often on CNN. (See Chart 3.) As a percentage of the total time devoted to tax bill sources, the broadcast networks devoted 24% more time to pro-tax bill sources than did CNN (72% to 58%). Conversely, CNN devoted 62% more time to anti-tax bill sources than did the networks (26% to 16%).

Therefore, the imbalance between pro-tax bill sources and anti-tax bill sources was greater on the broadcast networks than on CNN. In other words, CNN, even though it still devoted more time to pro- rather than anti-tax bill sources, was nevertheless more balanced in its presentation of these sources than were the networks.

SENSATIONALISM

The second major finding of the study is that CNN was less sensational in its coverage of domestic business and economic issues than were the broadcast networks.

It may not be obvious to all that an increase in the degree of sensationalism necessarily means a reduction in quality. But, in fact, the use of sensationalism has this effect because it aims the news not at the intellect, but at the emotions. Or as one observer put it, sensationalized TV news "mainlines to the emotions before it can be filtered out and analyzed by the brain."5

The criticism that the news is too sensational, relying on drama at the expense of objective and dispassionate discussion, is not a new one. However, the recent recession, with its concomitant

---

5 Morton H. Kondracke, "South Succotash, Bang-Bang and TV News," <u>Wall Street Journal</u>, April 1, 1982.

personal impact, prompted one observer to claim, "the nightly message from the television screen is grim, heart-tugging and relentlessly depressing, the actors forlorn and pessimistic..."[6]

Lead-Sentence Analysis

During the viewing period, there were five days when CNN and the three networks had a lead story on the same subject. Based on these five days, independent research subjects participating in a "Q-Sort" test[7] almost always rated CNN as being less sensational in its opening sentences than the networks. On a scale where 1 was "very cautious" and 5 was "very sensational," CNN had an average ranking of 3.07 (straightforward); the networks averaged 3.97 (somewhat sensational). (See Chart 4.)

To understand how the analysis was conducted, consider one date, October 8, 1982, when CNN and the three networks led with the same economic story. This was the date the Department of Labor reported the highest unemployment rate in 40 years.

Statement 1

> It was not a surprise, but it was still a jolt --10.1%. And today, for the first time since before World War II there is double-digit unemployment in the U.S. 450,000 workers lost their

---

[6] Fred Barnes, "Network Coverage of the Recession," Washington Journalism Review, June 1982, p. 36.

[7] A "Q-Sort" is a research method used to measure attitudes toward various statements by asking subjects to place the statements along a continuum.

jobs in September and so now well over
11 million Americans are out of work.

Statement 2

The nation's unemployment rate now
stands at 10.1%. That's the highest
since 1940. We have a series of reports
on...a national tragedy.

Statement 3

Reaganomics took another body blow
today. Nationwide unemployment broke
10% last month. Broke it for the first
time since the tail end of the
Depression.

Statement 4

The Labor Department reported today the
nation's unemployment rate for September

Chart 4.

Lead-Sentence Analysis: Degree of Sensationalism

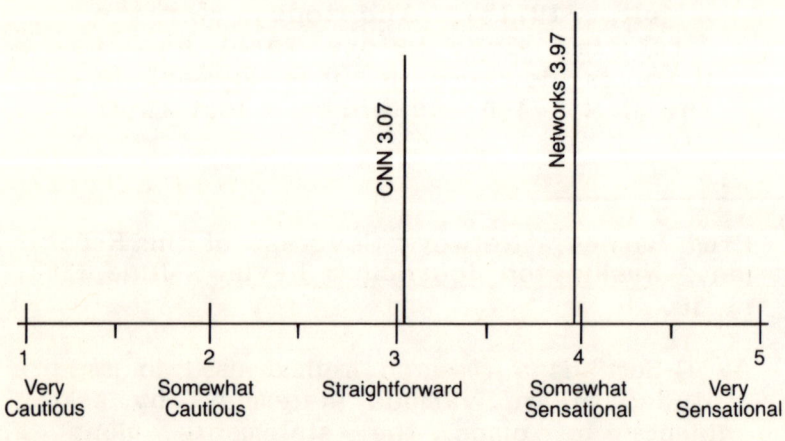

rose to the double digits--10.1%--to the highest figure in four decades. In real terms more than 11 million Americans are out of work.

The research subjects' average assessment was that Statement 4, the opening sentence from the CNN newscast, was the least sensational, almost cautious or understated (2.33). Statement 3, the opening sentence from NBC's newscast, was judged the most sensational (4.33), followed by Statement 2, CBS (4.00). Statement 1, from ABC, was assessed as exhibiting neither caution nor understatement, appearing roughly in the middle of the scale (3.33).

Case Studies

A principal criticism levelled at the networks is that they sensationalize economic news by focusing on human-interest aspects, or "case studies" of individuals--and in the process oversimplify, misinterpret, or even ignore complex economic trends and developments. Indeed, case studies are generally emotional in nature, and reduce the time available for objective and disinterested reporting of the actual event.

"On television a .2 percentage point rise in unemployment that might appear as an uptick on a chart or a figure on the printed page can become an emotionally powerful scene of unemployed workers and troubled families."[8] "For all their enthusiasm, the network news staffs still have a hard time telling an economic story except in terms of its impact on individuals."[9]

---

[8] Danforth W. Austin, "Media Get High Rating for Fairness, Less for Quality, in Covering 'Slump,'" Wall Street Journal, April 16, 1982.

[9] Time, "The Dismal Science Hits a Nerve," January 24, 1983, p. 68.

Indeed, during this viewing period the networks used case studies twice as often as did CNN, as a percentage of the total time devoted to business and economic news--10% to 5%. In addition, as a percentage of time devoted to case studies, the networks devoted more time to those that were negative in tone than did CNN--55% to 49%. Viewed another way, CNN devoted a greater percentage to positive case studies--40% versus 32% for the networks. (Negative case studies--which tended to be more sensational in the opinion of researchers--dramatized the unfavorable consequences of an economic development on an individual, such as a plant closing causing the layoff of a worker; positive case studies portrayed some favorable effect.) (See Chart 5.)

DEPTH

CNN's business and economic news coverage offered less depth than the networks' coverage

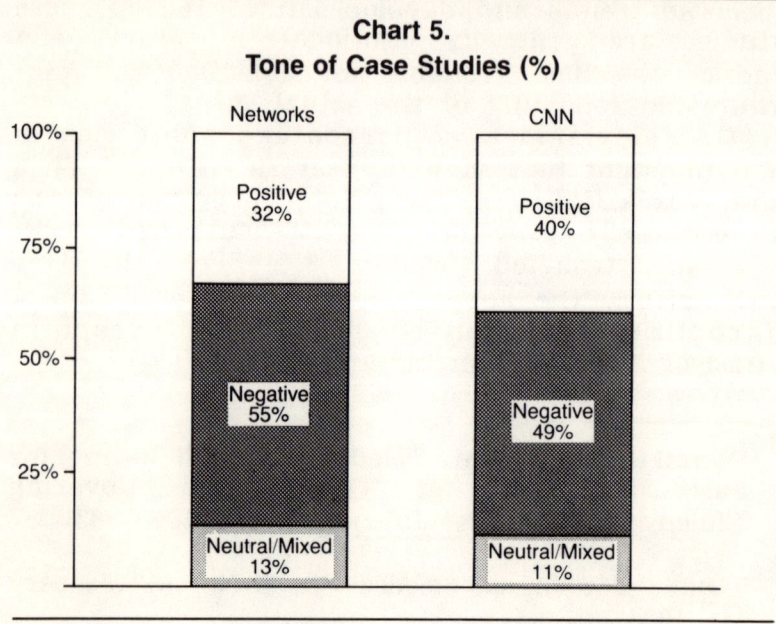

Chart 5.
Tone of Case Studies (%)

(relative to the time available), despite the two-hour format of <u>Primenews</u>. This is surprising, because depth is the criterion one might expect to correlate most strongly with the amount of news time available. CNN did surpass the networks on one of three measures used to assess depth, but the networks fared slightly better on the other two. On balance, this gave the networks a slight but noticeable edge in depth of coverage compared to CNN.

<u>Terms Explained</u>
One barrier to viewer comprehension is the preponderance of economic terms with complex or unclear meanings. "On all news beats, including the sports beat, reporters must understand and explain a peculiar lexicon, but the economics and business beat seems to present an unusually large challenge with a lexicon of such terms as fiscal policy, monetary policy, income policy, macroeconomics, microeconomics."[10] One can argue that if no explanation is offered for a business or economic term which is central to a particular story but not commonly understood (<u>e.g.</u> "liquidity crisis"), then the average viewer will have little more than a superficial grasp of the story's meaning and therefore its significance.

CNN, even with its time advantage, did not do as well in explaining economic words and terms as did the networks. During the viewing period, the words, terms, and phrases identified by researchers were used by each network an average of 24 times; four terms, or 17%, were explained or defined by each network on the average. On CNN,

---

[10] Laird B. Anderson, "The Broad Horizons of Economic Journalism," <u>Reporting on Business and the Economy</u>, eds. Louis M. Kohlmeier, Jr., John G. Udell, and Laird B. Anderson. (Englewood Cliffs, New Jersey:Prentice Hall, Inc., 1981) p. 6.

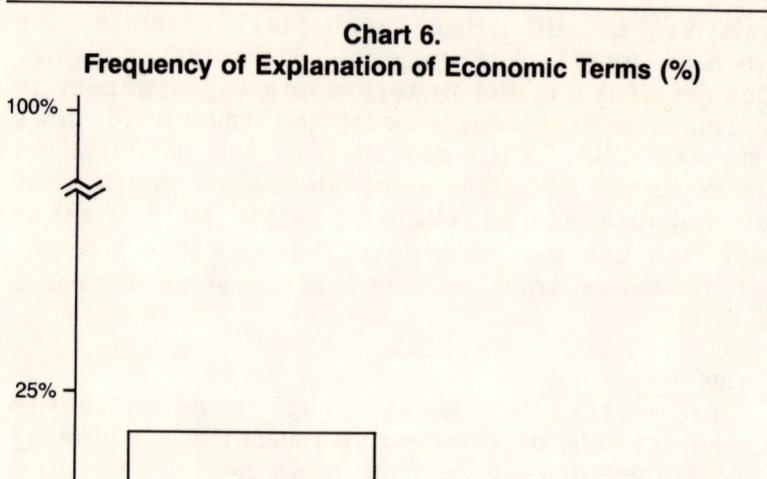

Chart 6.
Frequency of Explanation of Economic Terms (%)

the identified words, terms, or phrases were used 122 times, and an explanation or definition was offered nine times (7%). (See Chart 6.) A list of the identified terms can be found in the Appendix.

Stock-Market Rally and Tax-Increase Bill

The broadcast networks have also been cited for being remiss in discussing the background, impact, and implications of economic events and developments necessary for viewer comprehension. Economist Lester Thurow has named as one error of economic reporting, "...the problem of establishing appropriate background to help readers and viewers understand the significance of various news events."11 As another measure of depth,

---

[11] Lester Thurow, "Errors of Economic Reporting: A View From the Liberal Side," Washington Journalism Review, September 1982, p. 16.

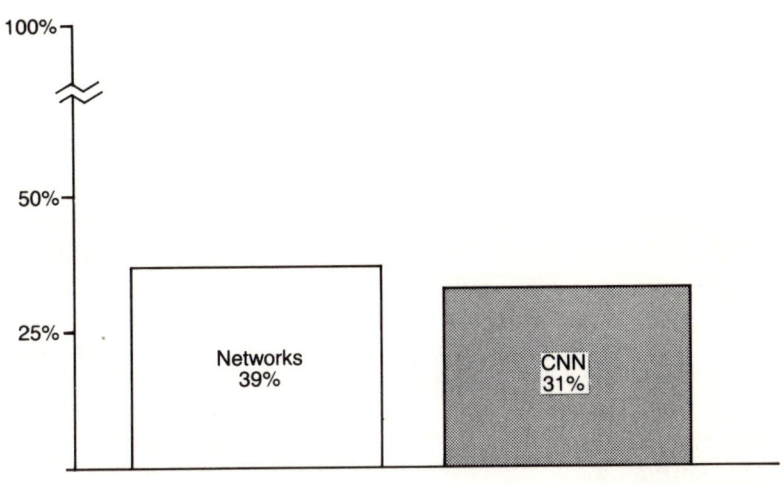

**Chart 7.
Stock-Market Rally News Time Devoted to
Causes and Implications (%)**

then, researchers analyzed the amount of time devoted to background information on two of the major economic events of the viewing period: in particular, the causes and implications of the stock-market rally, and the provisions of the tax-increase bill.

In this regard too, the depth of CNN coverage was no greater than that of the networks. In fact, as a percentage of total time devoted to stock-market-rally stories, CNN discussed the causes and implications of the rally less than did the broadcast networks--31% versus 39% (See Chart 7.)

The tables were turned, however slightly, in the presentation of background information on the tax-increase bill. CNN spent a slightly higher percentage of the time it devoted to the tax bill in discussing the bill's contents--2%, versus 1% for the networks. But almost all of the coverage, CNN and network alike, dealt with political alliances, ideological controversies and vote counts. In fact, only one network (CBS) spent any time telling its viewers what the tax-increase bill actually was--and then only on the day after the House of Representatives had passed it. It should be noted that CNN's discussion of the bill's provisions also took place after the bill had passed the House.

NEWS PRIORITY

No significant differences were found between CNN and the three networks regarding the priority placed on business and economic news. Once again, the measures used to answer this, the final research question, did not point consistently either to CNN or to the networks.

Percentage of Time Devoted to Business and Economics

The most obvious measure of news priority is the total time devoted to business and economic issues as a percentage of newscast time. Here the concern is not how the issues are covered, but how much they are covered.

During this viewing period, researchers found little difference between CNN and the networks in terms of newscast time devoted to business and economic issues. CNN devoted 20% of its total news time to business and economic issues, whereas the networks devoted 23% of their newscast time to these issues. (See Chart 8.) Perhaps we should note again that these totals are for general evening news programs only, and do not include CNN's other business/economic news programming.

An examination of the level of business and economic reporting on a week-by-week basis, however, reveals one curious difference between CNN and the networks: CNN was fairly consistent in the percentage of time devoted to these issues, while the broadcast networks were not. During the first week analyzed (August 17-20), a week which

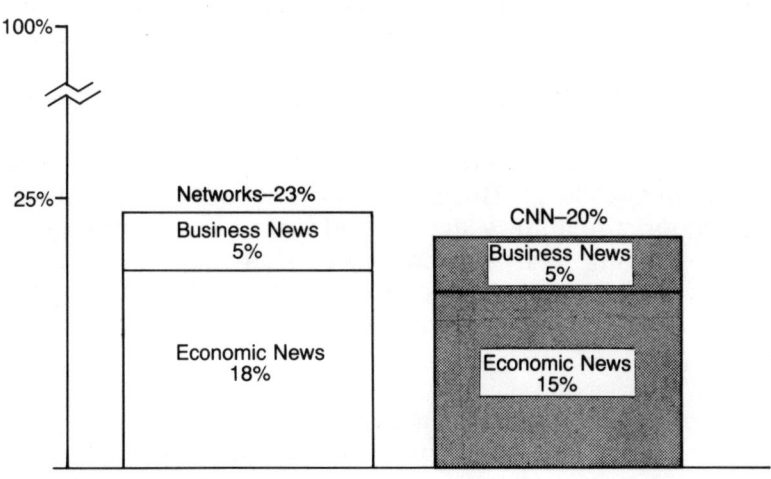

**Chart 8.
Total News Time Devoted to
Business and Economic News (%)**

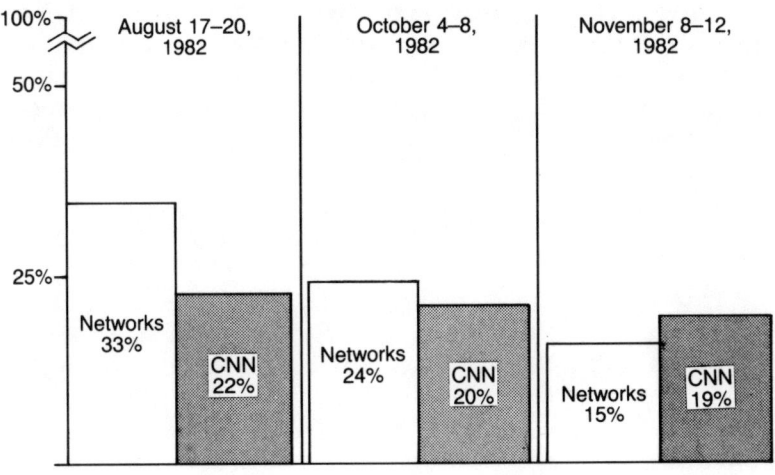

**Chart 9.
Newscast Time Devoted to Business/Economic News,
by Week (%)**

happened to include an unusually high level of business and economic activity, CNN devoted 22% of its evening newscast time to business and economic issues. While the second, and particularly the third weeks were less active for business and economic news, the percentages of CNN newscast time devoted to these issues remained fairly constant, at 20% and 19% respectively. (See Chart 9.)

Compare this relatively stable pattern to that of the networks. During the first week, business and economic issues accounted for 33% of newscast time. During the second week this figure dropped to 24%. During the third week this figure dropped again to 15%, less than half of what it had been the first week.

Rank of Stories in the Newscast

As another measure of priority, researchers also examined where in the newscast domestic business and economic news stories appeared, with particular attention given to those stories that ranked first, second, or third in the newscasts.

The study found that CNN ranked a domestic business or economic news story first, second, or third slightly more often than did the networks, but not often enough to be significant. CNN ranked a business or economic news story as the first, second, or third news item 17 times during the viewing period, compared to a network average of 13 times.

III. Comparison of the Broadcast Networks

While the goal of this study was to compare the domestic business and economic news coverage of CNN's evening newscast with that of the networks' newscasts, the study revealed some interesting differences among the three broadcast networks that warrant, at the very least, a brief discussion.

Thus far the study has compared CNN with the average of the three networks, which, given the broad goal of comparing the broadcast and cable media, was the most effective and fair manner of comparison. The following discussions, however, deal with the composition of broadcast coverage by individual network, and highlight only those areas where significant differences were discerned.

In general, ABC substantially outperformed CBS and NBC as measured by the study's criteria of balance, sensationalism, depth, and priority.

Time Devoted to Business and Economic Issues

ABC's coverage of domestic business and economic issues accounted for 40% of the total network time devoted to business and economic stories. This was fully 48% more time than NBC, whose business and economic news coverage constituted 27% of the total business and economic news time. CBS's coverage of business and economic issues accounted for one-third of the total broadcast time for these issues. (See Chart 10.)

Average Story Length
ABC had, by far, the longest average story length of the three networks. The average story (excluding short visual statistic stories) was 2 minutes and 19 seconds long on ABC, a surprising 72% longer than the average on NBC (1 minute, 21 seconds) and 24% longer than the average story on CBS (1 minute, 52 seconds).

Sources Used
Several major differences were observed in the networks' reliance on economists, business/industry representatives, labor leaders, experts, and men-in-the-street as sources of information.
Of the total time economists were used as sourc-

Chart 10.

Total Time Devoted to Business/Economic Issues, by Network (%)

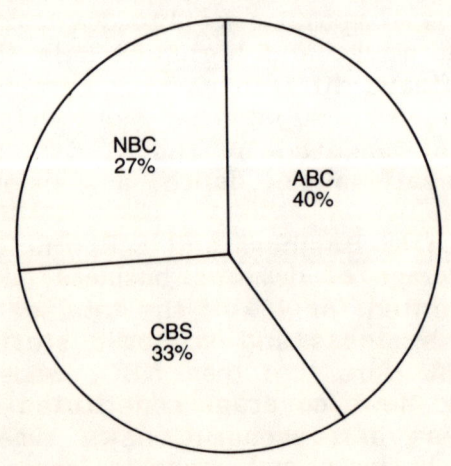

es for business and economic news stories on the networks, economists on ABC accounted for 41% of this time, almost twice the amount of time economists were used as sources on CBS (21%) and slightly more time than economists were used on NBC (38%).

Of the total time business/industry representatives were used as sources, they appeared almost half the time--49%--on ABC. That network used business/industry representatives virtually twice the amount of time of either CBS (26%) or NBC (25%).

Some dramatic differences were observed among the broadcast networks in the use of labor leaders as sources. Of the total broadcast time labor leaders were used as sources in business and economic news stories, ABC accounted for fully 60% of that time, 12 times that of NBC (5%), and almost twice that of CBS (35%).

Of the broadcast time devoted to experts as sources, ABC again accounted for over half, or 53%, of the total time--almost seven times that of NBC (8%) and over one-third more time than CBS devoted to experts as sources (39%).

Of the broadcast time using "men-in-the-street" as sources, NBC ranked first, accounting for 41% of the total time these sources were used, almost double the time men-in-the-street appeared on ABC (21%), and slightly more than the time these sources appeared on CBS (38%). (See Chart 11.)

Time Devoted to Case Studies

Of the three broadcast networks, NBC devoted the greatest amount of time to case studies. Case studies on NBC constituted 41% of the total broadcast time devoted to case studies on all the networks, almost three-fifths more time than ABC (26%) and one-quarter more time than CBS (33%). (See Chart 12.)

Examining the case studies by tone of coverage yields a very interesting finding: CBS was the most negative and the least positive in its use of

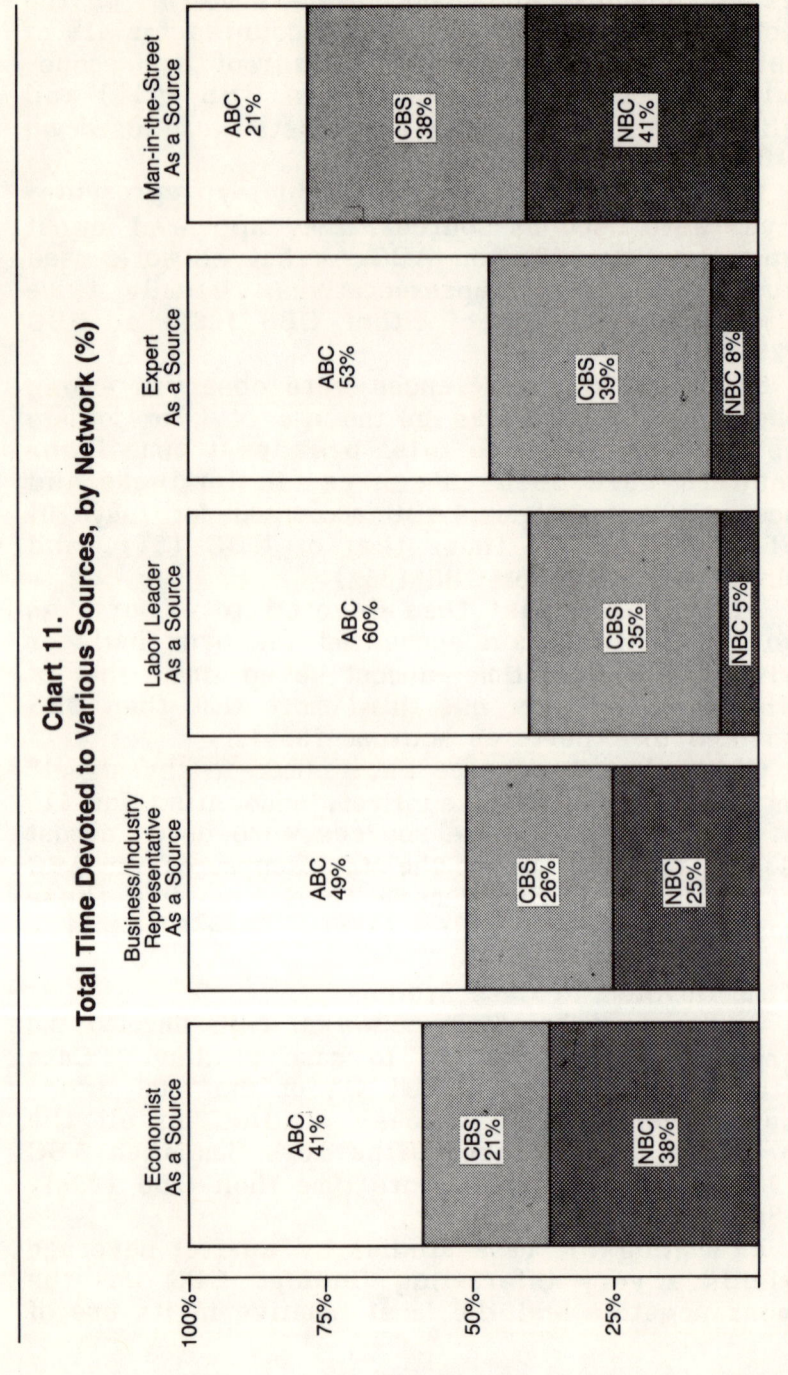

Chart 11.
Total Time Devoted to Various Sources, by Network (%)

case studies. CBS accounted for only 16% of the total broadcast time given over to positive case studies; this was about one-third of the time devoted to positive case studies by NBC (46%), and less than half the time allotted by ABC (38%).

Conversely, CBS accounted for almost half (46%) of the broadcast time devoted to negative case studies, over twice the amount of time ABC devoted to negative case studies (21%) and over a third more than NBC (33%). (See Chart 13.)

Time Spent Discussing the Causes and Implications of the Stock-Market Rally

ABC spent over twice as much time as the other networks discussing the causes and implications of the stock-market rally. Of the broadcast time spent discussing the causes and implications of the rally, ABC accounted for over half, or 53%, of

Chart 12.

Total Time Devoted to Case Studies, by Network (%)

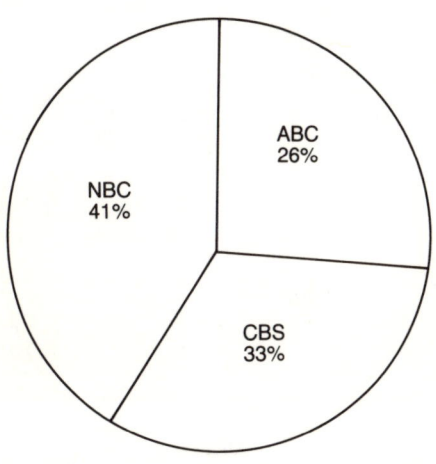

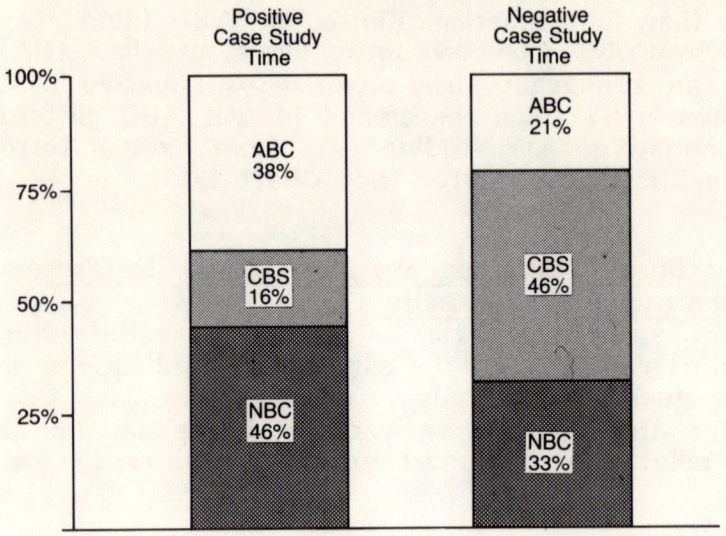

**Chart 13.
Total Time Devoted to Positive and Negative Case Studies, by Network (%)**

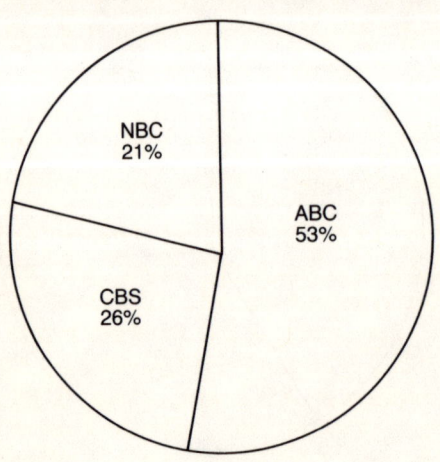

**Chart 14.
Total Time Devoted to Causes and Implications of Stock-Market Rally, by Network (%)**

the total--over twice the time of either NBC (21%) or CBS (26%). (See Chart 14.)

ABC Compared to CNN

ABC's superior performance vis-a-vis the other broadcast networks prompted researchers to question how ABC, clearly the leader in network business and economic coverage in its nightly news, would compare with CNN. Thus, researchers looked at a very limited number of criteria that yielded a number of interesting anecdotal findings. These findings showed ABC surpassing CNN in some respects, and CNN outperforming ABC in other respects. For example:

* Relative to the total amount of news time available, ABC devoted 40% more of its time to business and economic issues than did CNN (28% to 20%).

* As a percentage of the total time devoted to sources, ABC used an expert 42% more than did CNN (27% to 19%).

* Conversely, of the time devoted to sources, CNN used an economist as a source four times more than did ABC (12% to 3%).

* ABC spent a third more time discussing the causes and implications of the stock-market rally than did CNN (42% to 31%).

* But CNN, although it spent very little time discussing specific provisions of the tax bill, still surpassed ABC, which spent no time at all.

It must be stressed that these findings are merely anecdotal, because they do not reflect a comprehensive comparison of ABC and CNN, nor do they reflect any individual comparisons of CBS or NBC with CNN. It may be possible, for example, that CBS surpassed ABC and even CNN on a given measure, but it was not within the scope of the study to compare CNN with each network individually. The anecdotal comparison of ABC and CNN merely suggests that their coverage might be comparable, but is not comprehensive enough to allow conclusions about which network offers better coverage of business and economic issues on its general evening newscast.

IV. Background and Attitudes Survey of CNN Personnel

To gain a keener insight into CNN news operations, we undertook a separate research project in addition to the content analysis described thus far: a survey of the background and attitudes of CNN news personnel. In particular, we hoped to determine if and how these cable journalists differed from their network counterparts in their backgrounds, and their attitudes toward business and economics. (It should be made clear that the survey findings below suggest attitudinal differences only, and are not intended to show any kind of cause-and-effect relationship between the attitudes of CNN personnel and CNN story content.)

CNN complied fully with our request to survey individuals responsible for news content. We attempted to include personnel from ABC, CBS, and NBC as well, but the network news organizations declined to make their personnel available.

Instead, we used comparative data from a 1981 survey, "Media and Business Elites," by S. Robert Lichter and Stanley Rothman.12 These researchers,

---

[12] S. Robert Lichter and Stanley Rothman, "Media and Business Elites," Public Opinion, October/November 1981, pp. 42-60.

under the auspices of the Research Institute on International Change at Columbia University, interviewed 240 print and broadcast journalists at the most influential media outlets, including ABC, CBS, NBC, PBS, the <u>New York Times</u>, the <u>Washington Post</u>, the <u>Wall Street Journal</u>, <u>Time</u>, <u>Newsweek</u>, and <u>U.S. News and World Report</u>.

As part of a larger study of various "elite" groups in society, Lichter and Rothman ascertained the attitudes of these so-called "media elite" on a variety of social and political issues; the types of goals America should pursue in the next decade; and which leadership groups these elite felt should wield the most influence in American society.

Our study of CNN personnel was more narrowly focused, concentrating on attitudes toward business and economic issues. Some of our questions, such as those on the most important economic issues facing the United States, and the work and theories of economists, were unique to this survey. Others, including those on the role of government in the economic system, and social goals to be pursued, were replicated from the Lichter/Rothman survey. This mix of original and replicated questions allowed us to probe more deeply into attitudes on business and economics, while drawing comparisons with the "media elite" (and with a group of "business elite," as we shall discuss later).

Of the 109 CNN anchors, correspondents, writers, editors, executives, and producers to whom we sent the survey, 38, or 35% responded. Like the media elite, the CNN respondents were well educated; almost all (92%) had a college degree, and slightly over a third (34%) had completed some graduate work or received graduate degrees. Of the media elite, 93% had college degrees and 55% had post-graduate education. The average CNN respondent had over 10 years of experience in the news media.

ECONOMIC CONCERNS: PRACTICAL AND THEORETICAL

To gauge the general economic concerns of CNN news personnel, we asked a question that had not been asked by Lichter and Rothman: "What is the most important economic issue or problem facing the United States?" When this survey was conducted in fall 1982, a majority of CNN journalists (59%) rated unemployment as the most pressing economic issue. Inflation and the federal deficit were the next two most frequently cited issues.

Because we were concerned with attitudes on business and economics, we thought it would be helpful to gauge respondents' knowledge of economic theory. We asked the CNN personnel to identify, from a list of economists, those with whose works and theories they were very familiar, somewhat familiar, or not familiar at all.

Table 2.
CNN Journalists' Familiarity With Economists

	Very Familiar (%)	Somewhat Familiar (%)	Not At All Familiar (%)
Milton Friedman	60	37	3
John Kenneth Galbraith	58	39	3
Alfred Kahn	46	41	13
Arthur Laffer	46	22	32
Wassily Leontief	6	18	76
Alan Reynolds	0	9	91
Paul Samuelson	27	49	24
Leonard Tankersly*	0	6	94
Lester Thurow	26	19	55
Freidrich Von Hayek	6	8	86
Ludwig Von Mises	0	9	91

*Leonard Tankersly is not an economist, but a fictitious name included in this list as a control. To their credit, only 6% of CNN respondents were familiar with Tankersly, and then only "somewhat familiar."

Almost all (97%) claimed to be familiar with the works and theories of Milton Friedman and John Kenneth Galbraith, with a majority claiming to be very familiar. The next two economists who were most familiar to the respondents were Alfred Kahn (46% very familiar, 41% somewhat familiar) and Arthur Laffer (46% very familiar, 22% somewhat familiar).

Over 90% of the respondents were not at all familiar with the works and theories of Ludwig von Mises, while 86% were not at all familiar with the works and theories of Freidrich Von Hayek (who, like Friedman, is a Nobel Laureate in Economics). The respondents' familiarity with two other Nobel recipients was mixed: three-fourths were familiar with Paul Samuelson, but three-fourths were not at all familiar with Wassily Leontief. Fifty-five percent were not familiar with Lester Thurow. (See Table 2.)

ATTITUDES ON ECONOMICS

In the next series of questions, replicated from the Lichter/Rothman media-elite survey, the respondents were asked whether they strongly agreed, agreed, disagreed, or strongly disagreed with statements representing various attitudes on economics.

Almost all of the CNN personnel who responded (94%) either agreed or strongly agreed that people with more ability should earn more; this view was not held by quite as many media elite--86%. While 83% of CNN respondents felt that private enterprise is fair to workers, only 70% of the media elite shared this opinion. (It should be noted again that these media elite included both broadcast and print journalists.)

Differences in attitude became even more apparent on the question of whether the government should reduce the income gap. Almost three-fourths of CNN personnel--74%--disagreed or strongly disagreed that government should reduce the gap. By contrast, only 33% of the journalists surveyed by Lichter and Rothman felt the government should not reduce the income gap. Likewise, while a slight majority of the media elite (52%) disagreed or strongly disagreed that the government should guarantee jobs, an overwhelming 85% of CNN personnel opposed guaranteed jobs.

CNN respondents were most ambivalent about whether less regulation of business is good for the United States, but nevertheless a majority--57%--endorsed less regulation. Sixty-three percent of the media elite supported less regulation, making this the only instance in which the media elite displayed a stronger free-market attitude than the CNN journalists.

GOALS AMERICA SHOULD PURSUE DURING THE NEXT DECADE

In another question replicated from the media-elite survey, we asked CNN personnel to rank from most important to least important a list of goals America should pursue during the next decade. The response suggests the media elite are distinctly to the left of CNN news personnel in their socio-political outlook. "Maintaining a stable economy" received the highest rating from CNN journalists, followed in order by:

2. Maintaining a high rate of economic growth.
3. Fighting crime.
4. Making sure this country has strong defense forces.
5. Progressing toward a less impersonal, more humane society.
6. Seeing that people have more say in how things get decided at work and in their communities.
7. Progressing toward a society where ideas are more important than money.
8. Trying to make our cities and countryside more beautiful.

In this list, originally created by political scientist Ronald Inglehart, goals 1-4 tend to reflect traditional, conservative values, while goals 5-8 are associated with liberal values favoring social change.

A comparison of CNN personnel with the media elite found that CNN respondents more often selected traditional goals as their most important (84%) and second most important (78%), than did the media elite (most important 67%, second most important 51%).

Conversely, four-fifths of CNN personnel (80%) rated liberal goals least important, while 61% of those surveyed by Lichter and Rothman ranked these goals last.

Lichter and Rothman also compared the goal preferences of the media elite to those of 216 executives of major corporations. These corporate leaders placed a higher priority on traditional

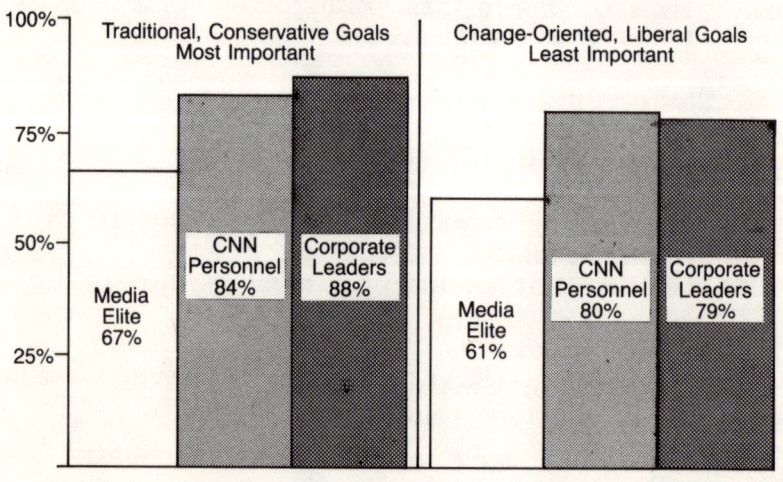

**Chart 15.
Choices of Most Important Goals for America in the Next Decade (%)**

values than did the media elite. Interestingly enough, the executives' ranking of traditional versus liberal goals was very similar (and in some cases virtually identical) to that of CNN personnel. For example, 88% of the executives and 84% of CNN personnel ranked traditional goals as most important; 79% of the executives and 80% of CNN personnel considered liberal goals least important. (See Chart 15.)

*   *   *

This ranking of goals suggests CNN journalists generally possess social values that are markedly more conservative than their media-elite counterparts--values that are, in fact, very much in tune with those of corporate America. This is confirmed by their attitudes on economic issues, where CNN personnel displayed a stronger preference for free-market policies and a stronger opposition to government-intervention policies than did the media elite. Based on these responses, it might be said that CNN news personnel are closer in attitudes and outlook to business leaders, than to their counterparts in America's most prestigious print and broadcast news outlets.

V. Appendix

A. Economic and Business News Categories

ECONOMIC

    Budget, General
    Budget Cuts, General
    Consumer Spending
    Corporate Profits
    Discount Rate
    Dollar
    Gross National Product
    Gold
    Housing Starts
    Income Tax
    Interest Rates
    International Economy/Trade
      (only if United States was mentioned)
    Mortgages
    Personal Income
    Prime Lending Rate
    Reaganomics
    Retail Sales
    Social Security
    Stock-Market Rally
    Stock Market, Other
    Tax-Increase Bill
    Taxes, Other

Unemployment
Money Supply
Other/Misc.

BUSINESS

Airline Industry
All Savers Certificates
Asbestos/Manville
　Corporation
AT&T/Antitrust & AT&T
Auto Industry/
　Labor Union
Auto Industry/Other
Beer Industry/Busch
　Boycott
Chemical Industry
Computer Industry
Copper Industry
Drug Industry/Tylenol
Drug Industry/Other
Fast-Food Industry/
　McDonalds
Mine Industry/Labor
　Union
Nuclear Industry
Nuclear Weapons Industry
Oil Industry
Retail Industry
Savings and Loans
Steel Industry
Television Industry
Other/Misc.

B.　Words, Terms, and Phrases Identified in the Newscasts

American Stock Exchange Index
All Savers Certificates
Base Lending Rate
Bearish

Bear Psychology
Block Trading
Blue Chip
Blue-Chip Issues
Bonds and Bill Market
Budget Reconciliation
Bullish
Bull Market
Bulls
Business Capital
Business Inventory Tax Reimbursement
Capital Markets
Central Bank Rate
Chapter Eleven
Commercial Paper
Common Stock
Consumer Installment Credit
Creative Financing
Cyclical Construction
Cyclical Expansion
Debit Market
Demand Accounts
Discount Rate
Dividends
Dow Jones Industrial Average
Excise Taxes
Factory Utilization
Federal Funds Rate
Federal Reserve Board
Fund-Rate Mortgage
Flat Tax Rate
Flexible Monetary Policy
Gross National Product
Growth Target
Home Loan Bank Board
Infrastructure
Institutional Investors
Inventory-to-Sales Ratio
Lagging Indicator
Leading Economic Indicators
Letter of Credit
Liquidity

Liquidity Crisis
Loan Demand
Long-Term Interest Rates
Long-Term Corporate Bond Flotations
M1
Mature
Money Market Funds
Money Supply
Mortgage Delinquency Rate
National Debt
New Dealers
NASDAQ
New York Stock Exchange Index
Paper Value
Personal Income
Personal Spending
Primary Inquiry
Prime Rate
Private Investors
Rate of Exchange
Rate of Return
Refinancing
Refugee Currency
Revenue Base
Service-Producing Sectors
"Shakeout" in Market
Short Covering
Short-Term Interest Rates
Short-Term Private Credit Demands
Short-Term Treasury Bill
Smokestack Industries
Trade Deficit
Treasury Bill Rate
Windfall Profit

PN 4888 .T4 C56 1983